CATFISH FISHING

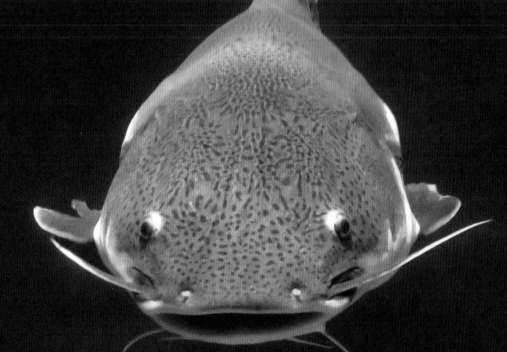

ROBERT Z. COHEN

rosen publishing's
rosen central®

New York

Published in 2012 by The Rosen Publishing Group, Inc.
29 East 21st Street, New York, NY 10010

Library of Congress Cataloging-in-Publication Data

Cohen, Robert Z.
Catfish fishing / Robert Z. Cohen.—1st ed.
    p. cm.—(Fishing: tips & techniques)
Includes bibliographical references and index.
ISBN 978-1-4488-4602-3 (library binding)
ISBN 978-1-4488-4605-4 (pbk.)
ISBN 978-1-4488-4736-5 (6-pack)
1. Catfishing—Juvenile literature. I. Title.
SH691.C35C64 2012
799.17'492—dc22

2010049934

Manufactured in Malaysia

CPSIA Compliance Information: Batch #S11YA: For further information, contact Rosen Publishing, New York, New York, at 1-800-237-9932.

CONTENTS

*B*ig, tough, and tasty, no freshwater fish captures the angler's imagination as much as the catfish. Catfish range all over the continent, from central Canada south to Mexico, and there is almost always good catfish water within a short distance of anyone who cares to go out and fish for them. You don't need fancy equipment or a hired guide to find catfish. From the small 10-inch (25 centimeter) bullheads that often live in city park ponds to the giant blue and flathead catfish that lie in the bends of the great rivers, catfish are just about everywhere. Cats are often the first fish that a new fisherman catches, and catfish offer everyone a chance to catch a real "big game fish" without taking a trip to the ocean. Sleek, strong, and perfectly adapted to its watery world, the catfish is a real evolutionary success story.

Mention catfish to many people and they may respond in disgust: Ugh! It's ugly and slimy, has no scales, and has a big wide head and long whiskers! But beauty is in the eye of the beholder. When you pull a big catfish out of the water and it has a good look at you, what do you think the catfish thinks?

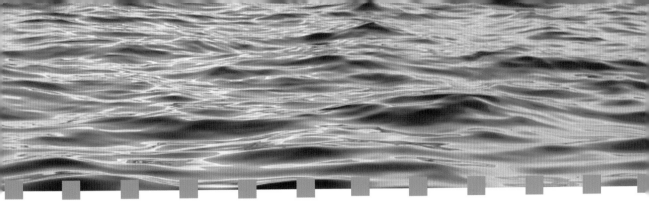

Catfish have played a big role in American folklore and culture, even before the arrival of Europeans. Among the Ojibwa, Odawa, and Potawatomi Indians of the Great Lakes region, the catfish is represented as the family totem of the catfish clan, Maanameg, and the bullhead clan, Wawaazisii, which are charged with educating and mediating disputes between chiefs. In Japan, catfish are feared and rarely eaten, since it is believed that the giant catfish called Namazu is the cause of earthquakes. Catfish were very important to African Americans in the southern United States as a food fish and as a symbol of strength during the period of slavery and later. Folk songs are still sung about the wily and tough catfish. "Catfish" also became a common nickname. New York Yankee baseball pitcher Catfish Hunter and the influential funk guitarist Catfish Collins are rarely remembered by their proper names—James and Phelps—anymore.

One reason so many fishermen love catfish is that they are often the first fish a young fisherman catches. Catching catfish is only a part of the fishing experience. Good fishermen enter into the world of the fish and imagine themselves in the mind-set of the creature at the other end of the fishing line. Fishing is like the meeting of two alien worlds: one perfectly adapted to the underwater environment, the other—you—always learning more about it. And as we come to appreciate our prey, we come to appreciate our environment and all that we need to do to preserve it for future generations to enjoy as we do.

With catfish you have to be prepared for just about anything. When you feel the first taps that tell you a fish has taken your bait you could be into a 10-inch (25 cm) bullhead or a 12-pound (5.4 kilogram) flathead—you won't know till you get it in the net. Every catfish feels like a big one when you first start reeling it in. In 2009, an English girl named Jessica Wanstall was out fishing with her family on the Ebro River in Spain. She landed a 9-foot-long (2.7 meter), 193-pound (87.5 kg) European wels catfish after a twenty-minute struggle. Jessica won the European record for any freshwater fish caught in Europe by a child. She was eleven years old.

CHAPTER 1

GOOD FISHING
IS SAFE FISHING

Fishing is one of the safest outdoor activities, but accidents can always happen. The fishing environment, whether standing on a riverbank or sitting cramped in a small boat, can seem like an alien world to a beginning fisherman. Remember: You are out fishing for fun, not survival, so take precautions to ensure that you fish safely. Safe fishing is successful fishing. Take the time to learn how to handle your fishing tackle with skill and confidence. The fishing environment is not like the world you know at home—it requires care and preparation to master.

Grab Your Gear!

Fishing is a messy activity, so dress in clothes that you won't mind getting dirty. Fishing on the shores of a lake or river can mean getting muddy or wet.

Standing around all day in wet shoes or sneakers isn't fun, so many fishermen choose to wear rubber boots that reach up to the knee and have rubber cleats that prevent slipping. Be wary about stepping into the water. Catfish often live in rivers with strong currents that can sweep an unsuspecting wader off his or her feet. If you are knee-deep in the water, stepping into hidden holes and sunken logs can send you tumbling into the water even inches from the shore.

Whether in a boat or on the shore, a hat provides protection from the sun, and it's a good idea to take along sunblock to prevent sunburn. The light reflecting off the surface of the water increases the chance of painful sunburn, which can affect you even though it is not summer. A good pair of polarized sunglasses protects your eyes and helps you see below the glare of the surface water.

Pack a light raincoat or poncho in case the weather changes. Fishing can often be good during a light rain, but at the first sign of a thunderstorm, it is best to retreat to some dry shelter. Never sit under a tall tree, which can attract lightning. Modern graphite fishing rods can act as lightning rods, so it's best to break them down and wait out a bad storm.

Don't leave home without a good brand of insect repellent. The waterside attracts all sorts of small insect pests, including mosquitoes and black flies, which can turn a good fishing day into a miserable experience. Avoid the cans of aerosol spray repellents and use the roll-on types. They are safer for the environment and lighter to carry.

You don't need to carry a lot of gear when you are out fishing. Keep tackle to a minimum and plan carefully.

Safety First

Always be on the lookout for animals that like to inhabit the transitional zone between land and water. Remember: This is their home,

Waterside environments are home to more than just fish. Snakes want to avoid you as much as you want to avoid them. When you see one, try to give it a wide berth!

and they may sense that you are the intruder and respond defensively. Poisonous cottonmouth snakes are common throughout North America and like to live alongside rivers and lakes. They are dangerous only if you stumble right on top of them and startle them. Snapping turtles can be a danger if you enter the water barefoot or if you attempt to catch and handle one, so it is best to leave them alone.

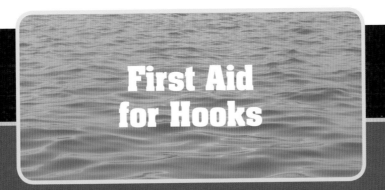

First Aid for Hooks

If you do get a small hook in your finger, the best way to take it out is to grit your teeth, hold the hook by its long shank, and press down to move the bend in the hook into the flesh. This clears the way for the barb to move backward. Then pull it out quickly. Dress the wound with disinfectant and bandage it. You don't want to risk infection by fishing with an open wound. For bigger hooks, it is best to head to the local hospital. Debarbed hooks (hooks whose barbs have been removed) are easier and safer to remove in accidents and are actually more efficient at hooking fish and make releasing them safer and less damaging to the fish. It is a good idea to carry a small first-aid kit on all fishing trips. Include items such as iodine (for disinfecting wounds), bandages, tweezers, and a small wire clipper for cases in which you may have to clip the hook.

Catfish water is often best covered by boat, which gives the fisherman a wider range but also means extra precautions. Always wear a flotation device in a boat and make sure it is securely buckled. Don't go fishing in a canoe or small boat unless accompanied by somebody well trained in handling these often unstable craft, and never stand up in a small tippy boat. Horsing around—whether on the shore or on a boat—is the number one cause of accidents on the water. If you do find yourself in the water, your priorities are to save yourself and get onto dry land, not to hold on to your fishing rod.

Your fishing tackle requires some special care to handle it safely. Fishing rods should be transported unassembled and then put together at the fishing spot. Walking through the woods with a fully rigged catfish rod can lead to a broken rod. If you must carry a fully rigged rod through heavy brush, make sure you are not near any fishing friends who can get poked by the sharp tip of your rod.

A good pocket utility knife has many uses during a fishing trip, whether for opening cans, preparing bait, cutting lines, or preparing the catch for dinner. Remember, knives are not toys, and you should always keep safety in mind when using one. Learn to sharpen your knife well on a sharpening stone. Most knife accidents occur because a dull blade needs more pressure to cut than a sharp one. Always hand a knife to somebody else with the handle first, and remember to close the blade by folding it between the open palms of your hands, not by holding the blade by your fingers.

Fishhooks for catfish can be small or large, but always handle them with care. The most common mishaps are pricking your finger while tying a knot and snagging a hook on yourself while making a cast. When tying knots or baiting a hook, always be aware of where your line is so that you don't accidentally get yourself or your friend snared in the line with a sharp hook at the end.

PALOMAR KNOT

IMPROVED CLINCH

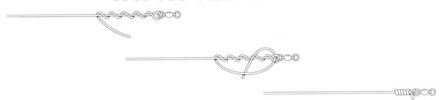

SURGEON'S KNOT

THE DROPPER LOOP

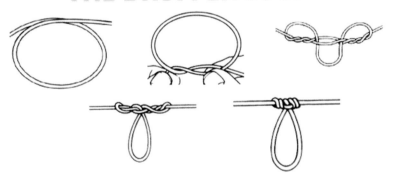

Being able to tie a good knot is an important skill for any fisherman. The Palomar, improved clinch, and surgeon's knot are all popular knots for tying a hook to a line, and the dropper loop can be used to create a loop anywhere in a line.

Knots

Get to know your fishing knots by practicing at home before you fish. Most fishing lines are made from smooth monofilament nylon, which requires special knots to prevent slipping. The most important knots are the following:

1. The improved clinch knot (for attaching hooks or lures to a line)
2. The surgeon's knot (attaching two pieces of line to each other)
3. The dropper loop (creating a loop to which other rigs can be tied)
4. The Palomar knot (better than a clinch knot in lines above 20 pound [9 kg] test)

Catfish do not become spooked or wary if they see a heavy fishing line, so if you are going after larger fish or working in water with lots of snags and obstructions, don't be afraid to use a heavier line (up to 40 pound [18 kg] test) but remember that heavier lines require heavier rods and reels to cast.

Practice your casting without a hook if you haven't been fishing in a while or if you are using a new and unfamiliar rod and reel. Always make sure your fishing friends know when you are about to cast, and—especially when fishing from a cramped boat—be aware of where they are and take care that your cast does not come near them.

Tackle accidents often occur when your line becomes snagged in the water and you want to retrieve your valuable bait or lure. If you fish for catfish, your hook and line will get caught on rocks or submerged tree trunks. In these cases, do not try to free the line by tugging up on the rod—rods can, and do, break. Grabbing a thin monofilament nylon line and tugging at it with your bare hands is a guarantee for some nasty line cuts. So if you do grab the line, protect your hand with a cloth. If the snag is serious, accept the loss and cut the line.

Safely Handling Catfish

All catfish species have mild poison glands in the bones of their pectoral (side) and dorsal (back) fins. When threatened, the catfish stiffly extend these spines to prevent predators from eating them. The danger of getting stung is greatest when landing a catfish or trying to grab a small catfish thrashing in a boat. To avoid a nasty sting, carry an old T-shirt to wrap around the fish when handling it, and take care to avoid the spines. If you do get stung, the greatest danger is from infection: Clean the wound with soap and warm water, and bandage it. It may hurt like a bee sting, but if it swells, don't worry too much: catfish venom is very weak and wears off quickly.

CHAPTER 2

CATFISH OF NORTH AMERICA

The freshwater catfish is in a family of fish known in the Linnaean order by the Latin name Siluridae. Catfish are widespread throughout the world, having evolved after the breakup of Earth's continents over one hundred million years ago. North American catfish are mostly classified in the subfamily known as Ictaluridae, including over forty species of catfish inhabiting the waters north of Mexico. Most of these are small, minnow-sized catfish called madtoms, which are rarely sought by fishermen. There are several species of smaller catfish known as bullheads, and finally, there are the bigger catfish: the channel catfish, the blue catfish, and the flathead catfish. (Flathead catfish are actually members of another branch of Siluridae, the Pylodictus.) Within their natural ecological systems, large catfish are at the top of the food

Catfish "whiskers" are called barbels. These highly sensitive organs help the fish home in on its prey at night on murky river bottoms.

chain. Once they reach adulthood, they have no enemies besides fishermen and perhaps the occasional alligator. They are predators as well as scavengers, constantly on the prowl for food, whether alive or dead. Catfish have broad, shovel-shaped heads, perfect for maintaining balance and control in heavy river currents or for rooting for

Bigger catfish often stake out a hole beneath a submerged tree stump and lie in wait for dinner to swim along.

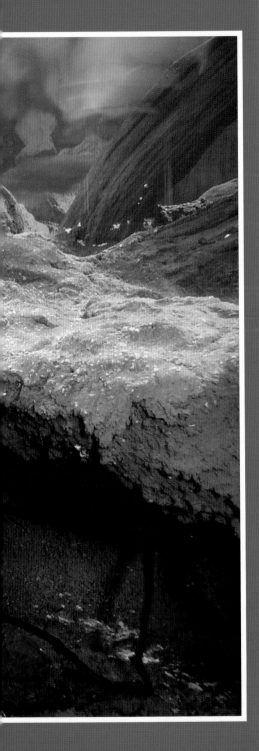

food on muddy lake bottoms. Catfish lack scales, and their bodies are covered with a protective layer of slimy mucus. Some catfish can even breathe oxygen through their skins and walk using their fins from one water source to another when faced with drought!

Thinking Like a Catfish

Every fish species occupies an ecological niche within the aquatic environment. Catfish, however, have evolved to take advantage of a broad range of water bodies and environments, with each species adapting to specific preferences and needs.

Catfish are especially active feeders at night, although during the day, they are alert to any food source and are willing to respond to bait at any time. During the day, catfish like to retreat to darker and deeper water. A good fisherman can recognize these underwater hiding places and increase his or her chances of success.

Catfish generally like big, slow-moving water with lots of cover. Small creeks and ponds offer no advantage to a large catfish, although they may be home to smaller bullheads and channel cats. Cats of all sizes like to hide in cavities that give cover and break up flowing currents, such as sunken trees, and behind large rocks. Taking advantage of the current, a catfish usually stays in one place with its head facing upstream in order to sense food sources flowing downstream toward it. Learning as much as we can about the feeding habits of the fish and its behavior patterns are the keys to fishing success.

Catfish spawn when the water warms between late spring and early summer. Unlike many animal parents, the male catfish plays the main role in taking care of the eggs and young catfish. The male catfish finds a small cave or hollow log and cleans it out, and after the female lays her eggs, the male drives her away and stays to protect the eggs from hungry fish who would love to dine on a catfish omelet. Even after the eggs have hatched into baby "fingerling" catfish, the father catfish remains on guard.

The Catfish's Senses

Fish in the catfish family all have small eyes, which are perfectly suited for the dim and murky water in which they often live. Channel catfish, however, have particularly good vision and are even used by medical centers for research in vision. The channel catfish live in clearer waters, and unlike other catfish, they may be caught on artificial lures or flies that are attractive only to sharp-sighted fish.

What the catfish lack in vision, they more than make up for with a spectacular sense of taste and smell. A catfish is so sensitive to taste that it is like a giant tongue. Catfish have cells much like taste buds all over their bodies. A 6-inch (15 cm) catfish may have more than a quarter million taste buds on its body. The catfish's barbels, or whiskers, are even more densely packed with taste receptors, as well as being highly sensitive to vibrations in the water. Taste alerts the catfish to the presence of food—alive or dead—in the water. Closely related to taste is the catfish's sense of smell. A catfish's nostrils have special folds that alert it to subtle nuances of aroma in the water flowing toward it. A channel cat has 180 folds in its nostrils, while a trout has 18, and a bass only 10. Catfish can sense a meal from far away, and they can sense strange and unpleasant smells, such as gasoline, insect repellent, and tobacco. Be careful when handling your bait and tackle—the fish will be able to smell you and may become alarmed.

They may have small eyes, but catfish have a keen sense of sight to complement their amazing arsenal of senses.

Catfish have a peculiarly acute sense of hearing. All fish have a special organ called a lateral line along their bodies to sense low frequency sounds and vibrations. Catfish, however, also have a resonant swim bladder—the organ that controls a fish's floating ability—that is directly connected to tiny bones (called otoliths) in their ears. Trout or bass can hear sound vibrations from about twenty to one thousand cycles per second. Catfish hearing is much more acute, sensing up to thirteen thousand cycles per second.

Most amazingly, catfish are able to sense the electric fields given off by living creatures. Their heads are covered in tiny cells that act like radar, responding to faint electric signals. This sense, known as electroreception, allows catfish to sense small creatures like insects and baby fish as they root into the muddy bottom of rivers and lakes, but it is only effective in very close range.

The Bullheads

Bullheads (called "horned pout" in some areas of the United States and Canada) are smaller catfish that are rarely larger than 16 inches (41 cm) in length. Bullheads live and feed mostly on the bottoms of lakes, ponds, and slow-flowing rivers and streams. The current world record for a bullhead is 6 pounds 5 ounces (2.86 kg), caught in Lake Mahopac, New York, in 2002. The most common is the brown bullhead (*Ameiurus nebulosus*), but the smaller yellow and black bullheads all share similar habits. Technically a bullhead, the white catfish (*Ameiurus catus*) is somewhat larger and behaves more like a channel catfish. Bullheads are tolerant of warm or even heavily polluted water. They prowl the muddy bottom scavenging for food, living or dead. Aquatic insects, crustaceans, dead fish, and even plants and algae make up a bullhead's diet. The lessons learned from fishing and catching bullheads help fishermen as they move up to fishing for the bullhead's larger catfish cousins.

Giant Cats

Elsewhere in the world catfish can grow to giant sizes. The world record is 646 pounds (293 kg)—over 9 feet (2.7 m) long—for the Mekong giant catfish of Southeast Asia. This species is now critically endangered, and efforts are under way to breed Mekong catfish eggs in an effort to save the species from extinction. In Europe, the giant wels catfish is a popular food and sport fish living in large rivers and lakes. The largest giant wels catfish recorded is 203 pounds (92 kg), but larger fish up to 300 pounds (136 kg) have been reported. The scariest may be the goonch catfish, which lives in the cold waters of the upper Ganges River in India. Growing to over 6 feet (1.8 m) in length and upward of 160 pounds (73 kg), the goonch is a voracious feeder. Between 1998 and 2007, several young swimmers disappeared while swimming in the Ganges near Nepal, and it is suspected that goonch catfish, having developed a taste for humans, were responsible.

Channel Catfish

The channel catfish (*Ictalurus punctatus*) is the single most sought after game fish of the catfish family. Sleek and strong, the channel catfish averages 3 to 5 pounds (1.4 to 2.3 kg). The world-record channel catfish, pulled from the Santee-Cooper Reservoir in South Carolina in 1964, weighed 58 pounds (26.3 kg). Channel catfish like clear, clean water and live in large lakes and flowing rivers. They can also be found in cold water such as trout streams. Channel catfish seek out sheltered areas such as hollow logs or old muskrat holes in which to hide. Channel cats

Big catfish will eat just about anything that they can sense in the water—including things that are dead and decaying—but they prefer fresh fish.

will eat insects, crayfish, plants, and even frogs, but they are more likely to prefer fish and will chase their prey at great speed. Mostly active at night, channel cats often like to lie in the deeper, dim depths of a river (hence the name "channel" catfish) during the day.

Flathead Catfish

The flathead (*Pylodictis olivaris*)—sometimes called yellow catfish—are mainly carnivores and grow to weights of over 100 pounds (45 kg). The world record for flathead catfish was 123 pounds (56 kg), caught in 1998 in Elk City Reservoir, Kansas. It is the most nocturnal of all American catfish, feeding mostly at night. Like all North American catfish, the flathead lacks sharp teeth and uses its huge mouth to simply suck unsuspecting fish down into its bony gullet. Its size and feeding habits make it an unusual target for fishermen who like to catch it using only their bare hands in a form of fishing called "noodling."

Blue Catfish

Blue catfish (*Ictalurus furcatus*) are North America's largest catfish. Physically, they resemble the silvery channel cat, but they can grow much larger: the world record, caught on July 10, 2010, on the Missouri River, weighed in at 130 pounds (59 kg)! To grow that big, the blue catfish must be an efficient hunter. It will eat larger fish, especially bullheads, baby ducks, and even small animals such as muskrats.

CHAPTER 3

CATCHING CATFISH

*E*very fisherman needs the right equipment to succeed. Luckily, catfish fishing doesn't require specialized or expensive gear. Many people still catch catfish using simple handlines, but a quality rod and reel will go a long way toward making you a better fisherman. Fishermen refer to their rods, reels, lines, and hooks as their tackle. A good all-around catfish combo would be a medium-weight spinning rod and reel that can be filled with monofilament fishing line between 6 and 20 pounds (2.7 and 9 kg) of test strength. (Test strength means the weight a line would need to break.)

Spinning Reels

By far the most popular method for freshwater fishing today is undoubtedly spin fishing. A spinning reel has a fixed, unmovable spool holding the line and a metal bail that is opened before making the cast. The fisherman holds the line on his or her index finger while making the cast and gracefully brings the rod forward, releasing the line by pointing his or her finger outward when the rod is pointing at the casting target. When the line hits the water, the fisherman closes the bail by turning the reel handle. Like most reels, a good spinning reel should have an adjustable drag. The drag controls how fast the line can be pulled off the spool. When a big fish takes the bait, it should be able to pull some line off the reel or else it may easily break the line. For any fish over 3 pounds (1.4 kg), a good drag is indispensable.

For bigger catfish, many fishermen depend on heavy-duty tackle and line. Sometimes it's even necessary to use saltwater gear in freshwater.

Baitcasting Reels

For the largest catfish, many choose to use a baitcasting reel and rod. Baitcasting reels sit on top of the rod, and the line is stored on a rolling spool. A crank handle operates the line retrieve. Somewhat trickier to cast, most modern baitcasting reels usually feature a level-wind mechanism, which controls the speed of the line spool to prevent tangling during casts. Larger baitcasting rods are more effective at bringing up large fish from the bottom of rivers with strong currents, making them a favorite of those who target larger flathead and blue catfish.

Spincasting Reels

Many younger and beginning fishermen choose to use a spincasting rod and reel combo. An easy compromise between a spinning rod and a light baitcasting rod, spincasting reels have a cover over the line spool. Instead of using the index finger to control the cast, there is a simple button or lever that is pushed and released. Spincasting is fine for smaller catfish such as bullheads and for panfish such as sunfish and perch.

Other Methods

Catfish are caught by a variety of other methods. Fly fishermen rarely catch catfish because they rarely use natural bait. But in recent years, more and more fly fishermen have targeted sharp-eyed channel cats, especially those that inhabit the clear tailwaters downstream of reservoir dams. In places where it is legal, many people still set "trot lines" for catfish. These are set lines hung between trees, poles, or floats that hang over the water, and shorter drop lines are baited every few feet. These are set out overnight, and the fishermen check the lines in the morning for any catfish hooked during the night.

Noodling for Cats

Some people keep things simple: they catch large catfish with their bare hands! In Arkansas and Oklahoma, this form of fishing has been developed into a special sport called "noodling for catfish." A team of two people, a spotter and a catcher, dive into the water feeling around with their hand for the holes and cavities that flathead catfish—which like to stay in one place—inhabit. When the catfish

is surprised, it clamps down on the noodler's fist. The noodler then wrestles the fish to the surface. It can be dangerous to wrestle a 60-pound (27 kg) flathead to the surface, but since the flathead has no teeth, the noodler usually suffers only a bruise. Noodling has become so popular in the South that the Okie Noodling Festival is held annually at Pauls Valley, Oklahoma, south of Oklahoma City. In 2010, it attracted over 170 participants.

Catfish noodlers work in teams to ensure safety. Once done only to provide food, noodling has now become famous as an extreme sport!

Basic Rigs for Bullheads

Bullheads are often the first catfish most beginners catch, and the techniques used will go a long way to preparing you for catching the larger cats. Like most catfish, bullheads feed mostly on the bottom, and they are almost always caught on bait, rarely on artificial lures. The best baits by far are garden worms and the larger worms called night crawlers. In June and July, crayfish are a great bullhead bait as well—you can

A favorite catfish bait is a fat night crawler. Even after it's hooked through, the worm can remain alive and lively for a long time.

catch them by hanging a piece of chicken neck in the water on a string and carefully pulling it up.

A 6- to 10-pound (2.7 to 4.5 kg) test monofilament line will handle most bullhead situations. Hooks can be relatively large—between size 6 and size 1—and long-shanked, since a bullhead will typically swallow a bait deep, making hook removal difficult. One remedy for this is to use newly designed, short-shanked circle hooks, which won't hook into a fish's gullet.

A good basic terminal, or end of the line, rig for bullheads is the "slip rig" using a small oval-shaped sliding sinker. Crimp on a small split-shot sinker to the line about 1 foot (30.5 cm) above the hook to prevent the sinker from sliding all the way to the hook. This will allow the bait to rest on the bottom, but when a fish takes the bait, it can move with the line without feeling the weight of the heavy sinker. Many fish will spit out bait prematurely if they feel weight. Let the fish run with the bait for a few seconds, then take in your slack line and lift the rod to set the hook firmly.

Basic Tackle for Larger Cats

Channel cats and white cats are opportunistic feeders just like bullheads. If targeting larger channel cats, use a medium-weight spinning rod and 10-pound (4.5 kg) test line to deal with the kind of snags and obstacles that are often found in channel cat water.

Channel cats will eat almost anything. Once a fish grows to more than 20 inches (51 cm), however, it increasingly depends on live fish for food. While usually seeking out deeper, protected areas in the water, catfish will often be found in different areas of a lake or river. Learn to read the flow of a river to find the deepest holes, undercut banks, and deep channels where the fish will lie and where food is easily available.

Channel cats, like all larger catfish, are active feeders at night, and some of the best catches happen after sundown.

Channel cats, and all cats, love big, juicy night crawlers. Minnows fished off a sliding sinker rig also lure a large number of cats, and many veteran fishermen swear by cut bait—a hunk of fish cut up and strung on a hook. Cut bait offers more enticing odors for the sensitive catfish to detect.

Aromas attract fish over long distances, and catfishermen have long sworn by "stink baits." Some are made from liver, chicken guts, fish guts, or chicken blood. Many recipes call for balls of dough flavored by liver, blood, fruit jam, and even vanilla extract. Cheese seems to work well in all mixed stink baits and is a good bet when other baits are passed by. Plain Ivory soap, cut into cubes, is also a favorite stink bait.

The Big Cats:
Blue and Flathead Catfish

For the larger catfish, you need stronger tackle. Heavy-duty rods, even those used for saltwater surfcasting, are commonly used when going after these behemoths. While all of the classic baits will work, blue and flathead catfish are usually sought using live fish up to 1 foot (30.5 cm) in length or larger pieces of cut fish bait on the bottom using a larger and heavier version of the classic slip rig. Some fishermen spend almost as much time catching baitfish as fishing for the catfish itself. Bluegills, sunfish, perch, and especially bullheads fished on large (size 2/0 to 4/0)

Night fishing requires special precautions, but the reward is a chance to catch big catfish that may remain inactive during the day.

hooks make good bait for large catfish. Don't expect a lot of fast fishing action when fishing large baits for big fish. It can take hours for a big blue or flathead to take an interest in your bait, but when he does, hold on tight! When reeling in a large fish, most fishermen use the rod to tire the fish out as it resists capture. By alternately pumping the rod upward to pull the fish toward you and then reeling in the slack line, you can gradually bring the fish to the net. Expect a big catfish to put up a fight that can last as long as forty minutes.

Fishing from Boats

For big catfish, many people use boats to get them out to deeper water. Special care is needed when fishing in a boat to avoid line tangles and to cast lines safely. Boat fishing for catfish, however, usually means the same bottom fishing technique that applies to most other forms of catfishing. Catfish do not actively chase fish at the midlevels of a waterway, so trolling (slowly fishing a bait or lure behind a moving boat) is rarely used as a catfishing tactic. Landing a large catfish in a small boat takes special skill, so be careful when that big fish comes to the surface!

CHAPTER 4

HANDLING YOUR CATCH

Catfish are an important food source in North America, particularly in the American South. Firm and meaty, catfish are an excellent food fish, and many farms have a special pond to raise catfish for the table. But you don't need to keep all you catch. In fact, many fishermen choose to release all of their catch unharmed on the principle that "a good game fish is too good to be caught only once." By using hooks with the barbs crushed down and a good hook removal tool, and handling your catch carefully, you can release catfish back into the water with relatively little harm to the fish.

Even if you do keep some of your catch for dinner, some catfish are better off being released. Catfish from weedy, murky waters often taste muddy, while fish caught in clear or

Many fishermen prefer to release their catch, and some even like to give the fish a good-bye kiss before returning it to the water.

flowing waters taste better. Large catfish are not as good for eating as smaller catfish: the best catfish for eating are under 10 pounds (4.5 kg). Large catfish are also the ones most likely to have picked up toxic chemicals in their fat and bones from water pollution, so it may be

best to release them to breed another generation of river monsters.

Whether you are keeping or releasing your fish, you will need a net to get it up a steep riverbank or into a boat. The truth is that catching a catfish is not very hard. The real work begins when you land it. Nets for catfish should be long, large, and stout. While many fishermen will simply grab a catfish by gripping its rough lip and jaw in their hands, you can use a special tool called a Boga Grip to do the same thing without the danger of hurting your hands. When taking the fish from the net or handling it on land or in a boat, take special care to avoid the sharp spines on its fins and back. Use a damp towel, work gloves, or a T-shirt to hold the fish.

If you do decide to keep your fish for food, the fastest and most humane method of dispatching a catfish is called "pithing." This technique requires skilled and confident knife skills and should best be done by an adult. Place a strong sharp knife directly above the head behind the catfish's two eyes and plunge it into the fish's skull, cutting into the brain. (Take extra care if using a pocketknife that you don't close the blade on your fingers.) This is quick and will save the catfish from unnecessary suffering. Catfish are very, very tough fish, and clubbing it with a big stick will often only stun it. Once the fish has stopped moving, keep it in a cool place—an ice chest, an insulated cloth fish bag, or even under wet cloths—until you can clean it.

Cleaning and Preparing Your Catch

Cleaning your catch—removing the inner organs, cleaning out the cavity, and skinning the fish—is best done as soon as possible, as fish can easily spoil. Start by cutting the stomach open from the anal vent up toward the gills, remove the inner organs completely, and discard them. (These can even be saved for future catfish stink bait.) Rinse the fish and take care to scrape and rinse out the dark, bloody spleen that runs along the top of the body cavity beneath the spine.

To skin a catfish takes some skill and practice—and a good pair of pliers. The easiest way to do it is to nail the head of the catfish to a tree or to a wooden board, letting the fish hang down. Cut the skin in a circle around the body just below the head and gills, and with a pair of pliers grab the skin and pull down. It may not all come off in one piece, but soon you will have a clean white fish ready for filleting.

Small catfish, such as bullheads, may not need to be filleted, but catfish have a delicate white flesh and a strong bone structure that makes filleting easy. Use a filleting knife with a long, thin, sharp blade, but any good knife will work. Place the fish on its side and make two slices alongside the dorsal fin that runs along the back of the fish. With a pair of pliers, you can now pull the dorsal fin completely out. Now run your knife alongside the body of the fish until it reaches the bones of the spine. Flatten your knife angle and slice carefully next to the bone, freeing the flesh from the ribs to the fatty area of the stomach. Use short slicing cuts until you have smooth, boneless catfish fillets. You can freeze your fillets in sealable plastic bags—catfish keep well in the freezer—or you can try any of the many traditional recipes for which catfish are famous.

Catfish on the Table

Most of the catfish we eat in North America are now raised on farms and fed on special catfish chow pellets. These farms are often in clean gravel quarries to avoid the muddy taste that a wild fish can pick up from living in muddy water. In 1987, President Ronald Reagan declared June 25 as National Catfish Day to celebrate farm raised catfish as America's third most popular food fish.

People need hydroelectric power, but dams on the Mekong River in Southeast Asia have brought the Mekong catfish—the world's largest—to the brink of extinction.

Catfish are important and popular as food around the world. In West Africa, they are often simmered with crushed pumpkin seeds in spicy egusi soup. In Hungary, they are stewed in paprika sauce and served over flat noodles as harcsa paprikás. In Thailand, catfish is eaten in curries, fried,

Fried Catfish, Southern Style

The classic way of preparing catfish in the American South is to simply roll the fish in cornmeal or crushed cracker meal and fry it in melted lard, bacon fat, or vegetable oil.

Catfish Fillets (4 about the size of your hand for this recipe)

1 cup (.45 kg) cornmeal	½ tsp pepper
½ tsp salt	vegetable oil for frying

In a large skillet or frying pan, heat ½ inch (1¼ cm) of oil over medium high heat. Place cornmeal in a bowl. Add salt and pepper, and stir. Dip and coat each fillet with the meal on both sides. Now turn the heat down to medium. Place each fillet in the oil and cook, turning once, until browned on both sides, about four minutes. Remove carefully and drain the oil on a plate covered with a paper towel. Serve with lemon wedges, vinegar, or tartar sauce—or the southern favorite for catfish, ketchup.

and in soup. The world record for any catfish was a whopping 646-pound (293 kg), 9-foot-long (2.7 m) Mekong river catfish caught in Hat Khrai, Thailand, in May 2005. Before scientists could retrieve the giant fish, the villagers decided the fish would spoil, so they butchered it and ate it.

Clean tasting, firm, and healthy, catfish fillet is perfect for people who prefer fish that does not smell or taste "too fishy."

Catfish, like most freshwater fish, should never be eaten raw due to the presence of microscopic parasites that can make humans ill. These are completely destroyed by the heat of the cooking process, but never experiment with catfish sushi or serve undercooked freshwater fish!

Remembering Your Fishing Experience

People who have caught a really big fish usually want something to remember it by. The best way to preserve the memory of a good fish is simply to take a photograph of it. If you intend to release your fish unharmed, try and handle the fish as little as possible, and take a photo of it while it is still in the water—there is no need to haul the fish up on dry land and put it through extra stress.

Some fishermen take their catch to a taxidermist to be mounted as a trophy fish that can be hung on a wall. This is a somewhat expensive process that requires careful preservation of the fish immediately after catching it. Today, many fishermen simply measure their fish, take a photo of it, and send these to a taxidermist who then molds a perfect plastic replica of the fish to hang on the wall.

CHAPTER 5

FISHING AND THE ENVIRONMENT

Healthy forests, clean lakes, and rivers where we fish are precious natural resources. Within any living environment, there are checks and balances that tend to control all living species in a way that ensures survival. This ecological balance allows nature to take care of itself quite well. We can see nature at work in the fish's world in something as basic as the predator/prey relationship of fish living in the same habitat. And we must remember that we humans are also a part of that relationship. It is our responsibility as fishermen to make sure that our presence in the natural world is positive and respectful.

As cities and industries expand and grow, it becomes more and more important that these wild and productive natural habitats are protected from destruction by pollution, overdevelopment, and environmental

Catfish can thrive even in severely degraded aquatic environments. Check with local fishing authorities to be sure to catch yours in safe, clean waters.

accidents. Fish and the water that they inhabit are not an inexhaustible resource. The giant Mekong river catfish in Southeast Asia is now considered severely endangered, prevented from reaching its breeding grounds by dams built to provide power and flood control for the growing number of people living along the rivers. Sometimes, human needs and the needs of fish do not go hand in hand.

Many fish that we depend on for food are in danger of possible extinction unless better fishing regulations can be agreed upon by the many different nations that fish for them. North America has seen the gradual disappearance of commercial fisheries such as that of the migratory Atlantic salmon, blocked by river dams from its breeding grounds. The once rich cod fisheries off the Grand Banks of Newfoundland collapsed in the 1990s due to overfishing caused by modern fishing nets replacing the older technique of handline fishing. Both sport and commercial fishermen, who are always the first to notice changes in fish populations, are among the most organized and vocal environmental activists.

Catfish, however, are a tough species that have adapted and evolved to the top of the food chain in a wide range of aquatic environments. They are one of the few fish in North America that have no danger of being overfished even with the increasing popularity of freshwater fishing as a hobby. In fact, by targeting certain catfish species, fishermen take the pressure off of fish species, such as bass and trout, that can easily be overfished by sport fishermen. Many lakes even encourage fishing for bullheads, which hungrily target the eggs of other game fish species and can easily take over a small bass or panfish pond.

Clean Water, Clean Fish

Catfish, especially bullheads, are surprisingly tolerant of living in water that is more polluted than most other fish can tolerate. They can often be found living in rivers that flow through built-up cities and in country farm ponds that may be full of chemical fertilizers from agriculture. While common bullhead are able to survive in polluted water, they may accumulate the pollutants in their bodies. Therefore, in some waters, bullheads contain higher levels of contaminants. Larger, older fish—over 20 pounds (9 kg)—are even more at risk from contaminants such

Modern methods of fish farming, or aquaculture, have made catfish one of the most popular—and sustainable—sources of fish consumed in the world today.

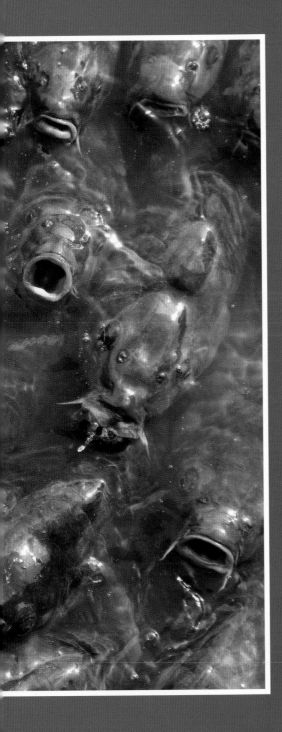

as heavy metals and PCBs that accumulate on the silt on lake and river bottoms. Always check first to see if it is safe to consume your catch from any water that seems doubtful. Your state or provincial fish and wildlife agency will often have a free pamphlet or a list on its Web site citing warnings for polluted waters.

Much of the catfish we eat comes from catfish farms set up in a clean rock or gravel quarry that has been adapted to catfish farming. Many offer recreational fishing for a small fee, often renting out rods and charging on a per-pound basis for any fish caught. This may not seem like the most sporting method of fishing, but it does guarantee a clean catch and has virtually no negative impact on the environment. And it is a great way to get the family out for a catfish picnic!

The Fishing Environmentalist

Fishing is a sport that requires an awareness of the natural environments that fish and wildlife need to flourish. Since a fisherman depends on the

Fishing clubs and environmental agencies work together to reverse the damage to natural environments. The mistakes of the past can be remedied by hard work today.

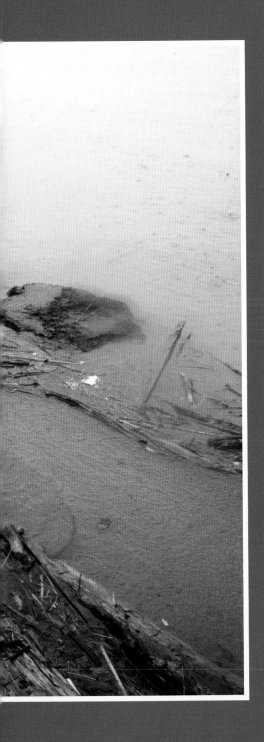

health of the natural environment to provide access to healthy fish and fun sport, everyone should do as much as possible to maintain healthy forests and clean waters. Always try to leave the woods or riverbanks with whatever you carried in with you. Bait boxes, soda cans, sandwich wrappers . . . leave nothing behind but your footprints. Carry a garbage bag with you and try to collect any discarded fishing line or empty bottles that you may find other less respectful fishermen may have left behind. You'll be surprised at how fast you can fill it up!

Fishing Clubs: United We Fish!

The future of fishing depends on the fishermen of the future, so start now to ensure that the fishing you enjoy will be available for generations to come. Joining a local fishing club is not only a way to get tips on hot spots and lessons on how to rig your baits for big catfish, although it may seem so. Many fishing clubs sponsor annual cleanups of rivers and lakes, even rehabilitating aquatic habitats in degraded rivers and lakes for better fishing.

Frankenfish

Any natural ecology is a delicate balance of species that grows over many years. When humans introduce a new species into the mix, it can lead to ecological nightmares. In the 1960s, the walking catfish, an aquarium fish imported from Thailand, escaped from tropical fish breeding farms in Florida. As long as its skin remains moist, the walking catfish can "walk" on its fins between different bodies of water, feeding on native fish and carrying a disease that can affect other native species. The disease that they carry is called enteric septicemia, and it is caused by a bacteria. The owners of catfish fisheries in areas of Florida that are affected by walking catfish often build special fences to keep walking catfish from entering their ponds and spreading the bacteria to the farm-raised catfish. Other exotic imports, such as the toothy Asian snakehead and silver carp, have begun to breed in American waters with no natural enemies. Even our native catfish can cause problems outside of their natural range: flathead catfish have been found in the Delaware River, and local fishing authorities encourage fishermen not to release any flatheads they catch. Flathead catfish do not naturally live as far east as the Delaware River. By not releasing these fish when they are caught, the fishermen are helping protect the many other species of fish that are native to the area. The common American bullhead was planted in European waters in the nineteenth century as a food fish. It soon became a problem, growing no larger than 6 inches (15 cm). Lacking native fish predators like bass and pike, it quickly overpopulates any water it inhabits, driving the local species out.

Local fishing clubs connect with larger environmental associations that lobby local governments for better environmental laws to protect waters from pollution and destructive development. Fishing is one of the most popular outdoor activities, and few politicians are willing to ignore the power of votes cast by concerned fishermen.

Many fishing clubs work hand in hand with state and provincial fish and game agencies reporting on fish populations, helping out with stocking, and reporting any violations of fishing regulations they may observe. The taxes and fees that come from buying a fishing license go to much more than merely providing stocked fish for anglers to catch. Environmental researchers are hired by fish and game departments to visit individual water bodies and test the waters. Fish counts are made to see how many fish live in a section of stream or lake. These are often done using an electric shocker that stuns fish but does not kill them. The dizzy fish float to the surface where they can be counted, but after a few minutes, they are fine again and swim away, leaving the scientists with a census of the fish population and a good idea of how healthy a water body actually is.

Becoming a Better Fisherman

In the end, fishing is not really just about catching fish. Fishing is about getting to know your fish. As your fishing skills develop, you become aware of the world at the end of your fishing line, a world much different from the world up here on dry land. You are actually communicating with a species that is as different from us as if it came from an alien world. You develop a respect for the fish and its environment, its needs, and its remarkable place in the natural world. This is what the old timers call "fish sense." After years of learning from our mistakes, from fishless days and missed strikes, chatting idly with other fishermen, and from reading fishing books and watching fishing videos, everyone eventually gets a sense of what it is that a catfish really wants. It wants something to eat—at a certain time of the year, at a certain time of day, at a certain point in the water. And at some point, you, the fisherman, suddenly get a sharp hunch that maybe a cast to that certain point in the river, by that bay in the lake . . . perhaps using a live shiner or a wad of earthworms for bait . . . and with an almost electric shudder your rod comes to life with the jerking take of a big catfish, feeling like a living earthquake on the end of your line.

And then again, there is the story of the one that got away . . .

aquaculture The science of growing fish in farms to provide a dependable source of food for market.

barbel A whiskerlike sense organ near the mouth of some fish, such as catfish, carp, and sturgeon.

carnivore An animal that eats meat.

contaminant A substance, usually a chemical, found in an environment where it does not belong.

crustaceans A Linnaean order of aquatic animals that grow outer shells as skeletons, such as crabs, lobsters, and crayfish.

dorsal fin The fin found on the top of a fish's back. The fins along the side, just behind the gills, are the pectoral fins.

ecology The scientific study of the relationship of living organisms to each other and their surroundings.

electroreception The biological ability to perceive electrical signals.

endangered species A population of animals that is in danger of becoming extinct.

fillet The slices of meat from a fish's sides usually cut so that there will be no bones.

fingerling A small, young fish.

gullet The throat of a fish.

Linnaean order A taxonomic system of ordering plants and animals into orders, genuses, and species, developed by Swedish biologist Carl Linnaeus in 1756.

lobby To try to influence decisions made by political officials.

monofilament A type of fishing line made from a single strand of nylon.

nocturnal Active at night.

PCBs Short for polychlorinated biphenyls, highly toxic chemical pollutants once commonly manufactured but now banned.

predator An animal that hunts and feeds on other animals.

rehabilitation To restore something, such as an environment, to its original state of health or purity.

scavenger An animal that feeds on dead organic matter, often other animals.

tackle A fisherman's equipment.

taxidermy The art of preparing and preserving the skins of animals for stuffing and mounting them in lifelike form.

totem An animal that is adopted as the mythical symbol of a family, clan, or tribe of people.

Association of Fish and Wildlife Agencies
444 North Capitol Street NW, Suite 725
Washington, DC 20001
(202) 624-7890
Web site: http://www.fishwildlife.org
The organization of North America's fish and wildlife agencies that
    promotes sound management and conservation, and speaks with a
    collective voice on important fish and wildlife issues.

Catfish Anglers Association
Web site: http://www.catfish-anglers.org
The Catfish Anglers Association maintains an online forum to share
    information between fishermen targeting catfish, as well as spon-
    soring regional fishing events.

Fisheries and Oceans Canada
200 Kent Street
13th Floor, Station 13E228
Ottawa, ON K1A 0E6
Canada
(613) 993-0999
Web site: http://www.dfo-mpo.gc.ca
Also known as the Department of Fisheries and Oceans (DFO), this
    government organization develops policies and programs in sup-
    port of Canada's commercial and sport fisheries.

Future Fisherman Foundation
P.O. Box 6049
McLean, VA 22106

(703) 402-3623

Web site: http://www.futurefisherman.org

The mission of the Future Fisherman Foundation is to unite the sport-fishing industry, a nationwide network of state outdoor educators, national conservation groups, and youth organizations dedicated to introducing America's youth to angling and the outdoors.

Greenpeace International

Ottho Heldringstraat 5

1066 AZ Amsterdam

The Netherlands

Web site: http://www.greenpeace.org

Greenpeace advocates environmental protection and education, and focuses its work on issues such as overfishing, commercial whaling, deforestation, and global warming.

International Game Fish Association (IGFA)

300 Gulf Stream Way

Dania Beach, FL 33004

(954) 927-2628

Web site: http://www.igfa.org

The IGFA is the largest organization regulating sport fishing and is the official agency that registers world-record catches of sport fish.

Ontario Ministry of Natural Resources

Fish Ontario

300 Water Street

Peterborough, ON K9J 8MR

Canada

(800) 667-1940

Web site: http://www.mnr.gov.on.ca/en/Business/LetsFish/index.html

Ontario's Provincial Ministry of Resources program for developing
    sport fisheries hosts helpful information about Ontario catfish on
    its Web site.

U.S. Catfish Association

Web site: http://www.catfish1.com

The U.S. Catfish Association is a robust Web-only forum that covers
    virtually every aspect of catfish fishing.

U.S. Fish and Wildlife Service

1849 C Street NW

Washington, DC 20240

(800) 344-WILD (9453)

Web site: http://www.fws.gov

The U.S. Fish and Wildlife Service is an arm of the U.S. Department of
    the Interior, which actively engages in conservation and manage-
    ment of wild resources, including fisheries. Extensive educational
    materials are available on its Web site.

Web Sites

Due to the changing nature of Internet links, Rosen Publishing has
developed an online list of Web sites related to the subject of this book.
This site is updated regularly. Please use this link to access the list:

http://www.rosenlinks.com/fish/cat

Amdahl, Paul. *The Barefoot Fisherman: A Fishing Book for Kids.* Broomfield, CO: Clearwater Publishing, 2004.

Baron, Frank. *What Fish Don't Want You to Know: An Insider's Guide to Freshwater Fishing.* Blacklick, OH: Ragged Mountain Press, 2004.

Beesley, Bradley. *Okie Noodling.* DVD film, 2001 (http://www.okienoodling.com).

Cheshire, Gerard. *Scary Creatures of the River.* London: Franklin Watts, 2009.

Crawford, Linda. *The Catfish Book.* Jackson, MS: University Press of Mississippi, 1991.

Dunaway, Vic. *Bait, Rigs and Tackle.* Windsor, CO: Wickstrom Publishers, 2002.

Finley, Lee. *Catfishes.* Neptune, NJ: TFH Publications, 2009.

The Freshwater Angler, eds. *Catching Catfish: The Ultimate Guide.* Minnetonka, MN: Creative Publishing, 2000.

The Freshwater Angler, eds. *The Complete Guide to Freshwater Fishing.* Minnetonka, MN: Creative Publishing, 2002.

Gray, Susan Heinrichs. *Walking Catfish* (Animal Invaders). North Mankato, MN: Cherry Lake Publishers, 2008.

In-Fisherman, eds. *Critical Concepts 1: Catfish Fundamentals.* Brainerd, MN: In-Fisherman, 2002.

In-Fisherman, eds. *Critical Concepts 2: Catfish Location.* Brainerd, MN: In-Fisherman, 2004.

In-Fisherman, eds. *Critical Concepts 3: Catfish Presentation.* Brainerd, MN: In-Fisherman, 2009.

Kugach, Gene. *Fishing Basics.* Mechanicsburg, PA: Stackpole Publishers, 1993.

Labignan, Italo. *Hook, Line and Sinker: Everything Kids Want to Know About Fishing.* Toronto, ON, Canada: Key Porter Books, 2007.

Morey, Shaun. Kids' Incredible Fishing Stories. New York, NY: Workman Publishing, 1996.

Samsel, Jeff. *Catfishing in the South.* Knoxville, TN: The University of Tennessee Press, 2003.

Stange, Doug. *Channel Catfish Fever.* Brainerd, MN: In-Fisherman, 1989.

Sutton, Keith. *Catching Catfish.* Minnetonka, MN: Creative Publishing, 2000.

Sutton, Keith. *Fishing for Catfish: The Complete Guide for Catching Big Channels, Blues and Flatheads.* Minnetonka, MN: Creative Publishing, 1998.

BIBLIOGRAPHY

Crawford, Linda. *The Catfish Book*. Jackson, MI: University Press of Mississippi, 1991.

Fishing Michigan's Upper Penninsula. "Cleaning Catfish and Bullhead." Retrieved Nov. 1, 2010 (http://www.upfishing.com/cleaning_catfish.html).

The Freshwater Angler, eds. *Catching Catfish: The Ultimate Guide*. Minnetonka, MN: Creative Publishing, 2000.

The Freshwater Angler, eds. *The Complete Guide to Freshwater Fishing*. Minnetonka, MN: Creative Publishing, 2002.

Game & Fish. "Understanding Catfish Senses." Retrieved Nov. 1, 2010 (http://www.gameandfishmag.com/fishing/catfish-fishing/gf_aa076502a/index.html).

Game & Fish. "Understanding the Catfish Spawn." Retrieved Nov. 1, 2010 (http://www.gameandfishmag.com/fishing/catfish-fishing/RA_0606_06/index.html).

In-Fisherman, eds. "Catfish Vision, Smell, Taste, Feel – Even Electrical." Retrieved Nov. 1, 2010 (http://www.in-fisherman.com/content/catfish-vision-smell-taste-feel-even-electrical).

Johnson, Steven. "Five Can't-Miss Channel Catfish Baits." Retrieved Nov. 1, 2010 (http://www.gameandfishmag.com/fishing/catfish-fishing/RA_0609_07/index.html).

Kehde, Ned. "25 Years of Catfishing Discovery and Innovation." Retrieved Nov. 1, 2010 (http://www.in-fisherman.com/content/25-years-catfishing-discoveries-and-innovation).

Kugach, Gene. *Fishing Basics*. Mechanicsburg, PA: Stackpole Publishers, 1993.

Samsel, Jeff. "How to Rig for Your Summer Cats." Retrieved Nov. 1, 2010 (http://www.gameandfishmag.com/fishing/catfish-fishing/RAhow_to_rig_for_your_summer_cats0710/index.html).

Samsel, Jeff. "Working the Current for Cats." Retrieved Nov. 1, 2010
(http://www.gameandfishmag.com/fishing/catfish-fishing/
RAworking_the_current_for_cats0510/index.html).

Stange, Doug. *Channel Catfish Fever*. Brainerd, MN: In-Fisherman, 1989.

Sutton, Keith. *Catching Catfish*. Minnetonka, MN: Creative
Publishing, 2000.

Sutton, Keith. *Fishing for Catfish: The Complete Guide for Catching
Big Channels, Blues and Flatheads*. Minnetonka, MN: Creative
Publishing, 1998.

Sutton, Keith. "Out There: A Baptism! Noodling for Catfish."
2006. Retrieved Nov. 1, 2010 (http://sports.espn.go.com/outdoors/
general/columns/story?columnist=sutton_keith&page=g_col_
sutton_noodling).

Sutton, Keith. "Tips for Bullheads." 2007. Retrieved Nov. 1, 2010
(http://www.outdoorlife.com/articles/fishing/2007/09/
tips-bullheads).

INDEX

About the Author

Robert Z. Cohen began fishing as a boy in the waters around his hometown of New York City. Although he has written about and fished for trout on three continents, he still finds the catfish the most fascinating of freshwater fishes. Cohen is a journalist, writer, folklorist, and musician. His largest catfish was a 5-pound (2.3 kg) channel cat, caught in the Quabbin Reservoir in Massachusetts.

About the Consultant

Contributor Benjamin Cowan has more than twenty years of both freshwater and saltwater angling experience. In addition to being an avid outdoorsman, Cowan is a member of many conservation organizations. He currently resides in western Tennessee.

Photo Credits